ideals® EASTER

Easter Day gilds all the land;
There's new life everywhere.
Resurrected are the flowers;
Their fragrance fills the air.

Chiming are the Easter bells
Both near and far away,
Ringing notes of hope and joy
This springtide Easter Day.

—LOISE PINKERTON FRITZ

IDEALS PUBLICATIONS

NASHVILLE, TENNESSEE

The Season Spring

Kay Hoffman

I watch the seasons come and go,
I hear the robin sing,
And in my winter-weary heart
I know that it is spring.

The little brook is chattering,
So happy to be free;
A daffodil in yellow dress
Joins in the revelry.

The flowers lift bright faces
In yards most everywhere;
The butterflies and honeybees
Are sipping nectar there.

The sky is turning brighter blue;
The lawn is sprouting green.
Pink blossoms on the dogwood tree
Fulfill an artist's dream.

As though this still were not enough
The weary heart to please,
The lilac spills her sweet perfume
Upon the rain-washed breeze.

I watch in awesome wonder,
Viewing winter on the wing,
And God in loving kindness
Sends the season we call spring.

Flowering dogwood and stone wall in Greenfield Hill, Connecticut. Photograph by William H. Johnson

from **Buds and Bird-Voices**

Nathaniel Hawthorne

Balmy Spring—weeks later than we expected, and months later than we longed for her—comes at last to revive the moss on the roof and walls of our old mansion. She peeps brightly into my study window, inviting me to throw it open and create a summer atmosphere by the intermixture of her genial breath with the black and cheerless comfort of the stove. As the casement ascends, forth into infinite space fly the innumerable forms of thought or fancy that have kept me company in the retirement of this little chamber during the sluggish lapse of wintry weather—visions gay, grotesque, and sad, pictures of real life tinted with nature's homely gray and russet, scenes in dreamland bedizened with rainbow-hues which faded before they were well laid on. All these may vanish now, and leave me to mold a fresh existence out of sunshine. . . .

The present Spring comes onward with fleeter footsteps because Winter lingered so unconscionably long that with her best diligence she can hardly retrieve half the allotted period of her reign. It is but a fortnight since I stood on the brink of our swollen river and beheld the accumulated ice of four frozen months go down the stream. . . . Never before, methinks, has spring pressed so closely on the footsteps of retreating winter. Along the roadside the green blades of grass have sprouted on the very edge of the snowdrifts. The pastures and mowing fields have not yet assumed a general aspect of verdure, but neither have they the cheerless brown tint which they wear in later autumn, when vegetation has entirely ceased; there is now a faint shadow of life, gradually brightening into the warm reality. Some tracts in a happy exposure—as, for instance, yonder southwestern slope of an orchard, in front of that old red farmhouse beyond the river—such patches of land already wear a beautiful and tender green to which no future luxuriance can add a charm. It looks unreal—a prophecy, a hope, a transitory effect of some peculiar light, which will vanish with the slightest motion of the eye. But beauty is never a delusion; not these verdant tracts but the dark and barren landscape all around them is a shadow and a dream. Each moment wins some portion of the earth from death to life; a sudden gleam of verdure brightens along the sunny slope of a bank which an instant ago was brown and bare. You look again, and behold, an apparition of green grass!

The trees in our orchard and elsewhere are as yet naked, but already appear full of life and vegetable blood. It seems as if by one magic touch they might instantaneously burst into full foliage, and that the wind which now sighs through their naked branches might make sudden music amid innumerable leaves. The moss-grown willow tree which for forty years past has overshadowed these western windows will be among the first to put on its green attire. There are some objections to the willow: it is not a dry and cleanly tree, and impresses the beholder with an association of

sliminess. No trees, I think, are perfectly agreeable as companions unless they have glossy leaves, dry bark, and a firm and hard texture of trunk and branches. But the willow is almost the earliest to gladden us with the promise and reality of beauty in its graceful and delicate foliage, and the last to scatter its yellow, yet scarcely withered, leaves upon the ground. All through the winter, too, its yellow twigs give it a sunny aspect which is not without a cheering influence even in the grayest and gloomiest day. Beneath a clouded sky it faithfully remembers the sunshine. Our old house would lose a charm were the willow to be cut down, with its golden crown over the snow-covered roof, and its heap of summer verdure. . . .

Thank Providence for spring! The earth—and man himself, by sympathy with his birthplace—would be far other than we find them if life toiled wearily onward without this periodical infusion of the primal spirit. Will the world ever be so decayed that spring may not renew its greenness? Can man be so dismally age-stricken that no faintest sunshine of his youth may revisit him once a year? It is impossible. The moss on our time-worn mansion brightens into beauty, the good old pastor who once dwelt here renewed his prime, regained his boyhood, in the genial breezes of his ninetieth spring. Alas for the worn and heavy soul if, whether in youth or age, it has outlived its privilege of springtime sprightliness! From such a soul the world must hope no reformation of its evil—no sympathy with the lofty faith and gallant struggles of those who contend in its behalf. Summer works in the present and thinks not of the future; autumn is a rich conservative; winter has utterly lost its faith and clings tremulously to the remembrance of what has been; but spring, with its outgushing life, is the true type of the movement.

On Planting a Tulip Bulb

Violet Alleyn Storey

Into my garden's heart, I put you now,
A clumsy, wrinkled thing.
When winter comes, share with my garden, then,
Frost and remembering!

Out of my garden's heart, when April's here,
Come slenderly and bring
A scarlet chalice, flecked with ebony
And lustrous with first spring!

At Winter's Edge

Alice Leedy Mason

At winter's edge
My eyes looked up to see
The mountains wearing
   snow continuously,
The frozen brook,
Each swaying, leafless tree;
And hope within my breast
Was chilled and numb.
With broken string
My harp of joy was dumb;
And I with fools would cry,
"Spring will not come!"

Then suddenly,
As flight of frightened fawn,
The mountains that were capped
   with snow at dawn
Felt the golden sun.
The trees reached out,
The brook had songs to sing;
And God looked down
To mend a broken string!

Photograph by age fotostock/SuperStock

Ode to Spring
Frances Kampman

An unseen warmth, a smile perhaps,
A gesture from the sky
Now melts away the blanket here
And shows the flowers shy,

Like bashful maidens who,
Afraid to lift their drowsy heads,
Have rudely been aroused
From deep within their winter beds.

Each blushing cheek is gently kissed
By spring's caressing breeze.

Not one enchanting blossom's missed
By honey-seeking bees.

A veil of misty green chiffon
Is worn by all the trees,
Who, tired of having nothing on,
Have dressed up as they please.

A lazy cloud goes drifting by.
A happy bird does sing.
For God, who heard tired winter sigh,
At last has sent us spring.

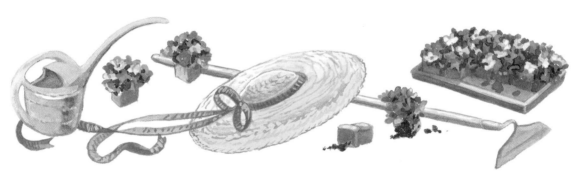

Easter Buttercup
Chris Dee

Little buttercup was wakened
From her long, deep winter sleep;
March wind had removed her blanket
With a sudden magic sweep.

Then the April breezes wooed her;
Softly they began to sing:
"You must have a yellow bonnet
And a fresh green gown for spring."

Buttercup stirred in her slumber;
Sunshine lent its warmth and glow;

Gentle raindrops bathed her rootlets—
Buttercup began to grow.

Every flower in the meadow
Knew the blessed story well:
"Christ the Lord arose in glory,"
Was the story they could tell.

On the blessed Easter morning,
Buttercup stood like a queen,
Vested in a golden bonnet
And in nature's gown of green.

Cherry trees and Mount Olive Church,
Door County, Wisconsin. Photograph by Ken Dequaine

Easter and a Silver Fork

Gail L. Roberson

I connect with Easter in my own way, in laying out the finery for the Easter gathering around the family table. My grandmother had such a large family that her silver was almost all handed away by the time it came my turn. I inherited her big silver serving fork, which nobody else wanted and I had asked for a thousand times. I didn't care about all the other pieces. I wanted that fork. You see, Grandma had used that fork, not for serving food, but for digging around in her garden just as Easter approached, year after year. I knew, as soon as I saw her slide it into her apron pocket, that Easter was on the way.

I'd follow her around in her beautiful garden, filled with colorful tulips and daffodils and low spreading pink phlox that ran rampant over the ground every Easter. I'd watch her push back a small area of straw mulch and stir up little spots in the soil with that big silver serving fork. Every Easter weekend, before she'd stick the ham in the oven or spread her white lace cloth across the huge oak table, Grandma and I would put some seed in the soil. She said it was her own form of resurrection, and that her faith, along with a little Easter rain, would have those seeds springing up and turning their blossoms toward the sun in a few weeks. In eastern North Carolina, winters were mild, and Easter always brought color and much-appreciated warmth, regardless if it was on the calendar for March or April.

One Easter, a surprise snow covered Grandma's little garden, but she still went out there with her silver fork and scraped off the snow, stirred up a spot of ground, and planted seeds. I stood beside her wearing my earmuffs and mittens and held the seed packets out to her. Sparrows had stitched a double row of tracks in the down comforter of snow that resembled the calligraphy of Great-Aunt Cennie's handwritten letters to Grandma. Our noses were pink when we came inside.

We always planted a seed packet each of marigolds, zinnias, asters, daisies, and dahlias and then tucked in a few big gladiola bulbs. We lived within walking distance of the little country church, and Grandma took it upon herself to grace the church's main tables with her flowers each weekend. We'd cut the long, thick stems on Saturday afternoons and walk the beautiful arrangements to the church for the Sunday service.

Today, I am the one testing and turning the soil with Grandma's big silver fork. I work in the velvet quietness of each Good Friday morning in my own little garden—much of which I moved from Grandma's house—planting it with the same seeds of spring and in the same manner Grandma once did. The fork, whose handle is encircled with a rose pattern, is sparkling clean and only slightly bent. It slides nicely down into the pocket of my garden apron. I also use it now to stir the soil in the pots of my African violets and orchids on the sun porch. It lies in its place of honor on the table by the door, ready for the garden at any season of the year. It would seem I have inherited much more than Grandma's big silver fork.

HEAVY DOWNPOUR *by Rollie Brandt.*
Artwork courtesy of the artist and Wild Wings

Spring Violets
Louis Ginsberg

Where heaven once on stems would glow,
Between the grass revealed,
Till violets had long ago,
Fading, unskied the field,

Once more does Heaven brim its blue
In meadows, now as then,
Where in the violets I knew
The sky takes root again.

Cycle of Spring
May Smith White

Nature's unmatched cycles lie in wait—
As buds sleep quietly through protected care,
Not fearing spring's last frost, which might come late,
Each bud lies shielded, yet quite unaware.
As in time past, true nature's flow is sure,
Always unfolding in her rhythmic way—
The early violet, shy and demure,
Is proof against those things that will decay.

We welcome spring that follows winter's hush—
Though silences brought calm that we might know
These ever-changing scenes from nature's brush
Are needed, like the brilliant afterglow.
With spring's true-patterned cycle we will see
White crosses forming on the dogwood tree.

Photograph by William H. Johnson

Bits & Pieces

To own a bit of ground, to scratch it with a hoe, to plant seeds and watch the renewal of life, this is the commonest delight of the race, the most satisfactory thing a man can do.

—*Charles Dudley Warner*

The most noteworthy thing about gardeners is that they are always optimistic, always enterprising, and never satisfied. They always look forward to doing something better than they have ever done before.

—*Vita Sackville-West*

A garden is evidence of faith. It links us with all the misty figures of the past who also planted and were nourished by the fruits of their planting.

—*Gladys Taber*

Ye flow'rs of spring, appear;
Your gentle heads uprear;
And let the growing seed
Enamel lawn and mead.
—*Author Unknown*

Far away there in the sunshine are my
highest aspirations. I may not reach them
but I can look up and see their beauty,
believe in them, and try to follow them.
—*Louisa May Alcott*

Of all the wonderful things in the wonderful universe
of God, nothing seems to me more surprising than the
planting of a seed in the blank earth and the result thereof.
—*Julie Moir Messervy*

Who hath a garden, he has friends—
Lilies and roses will not forsake;
When they depart, 'tis but for a time;
They will return when the spring winds wake.
—*Thomas Curtis Clark*

Easter Baskets

Faith Andrews Bedford

It is Easter Day, and the warm sunshine has finally coaxed my gardens into bloom. As my children carefully tuck tiny spring flowers into the bright paper baskets they will take to our neighbors, they beg me to tell them again the story of the years my sisters and I took Easter baskets to the witch.

Mrs. Pearson wasn't really a witch, but she lived on our lane in an old gray cottage whose overgrown yard was enclosed by a sagging fence. Her gardens, Mother said, were once the envy of the neighborhood. Now, we rarely saw her. At Halloween, she would place a bowl of candy on her porch and hide behind her faded curtains. When carolers came to her door at Christmas, her house remained silent and dark. But every year, when my little sisters and I made Easter baskets, Mother would urge us to take one to Mrs. Pearson.

Our other neighbors always made a great fuss. "Look, Arthur," Mrs. Peabody would call to her husband. "See what the fairies have left for us." Miss Addie Wilson, at the house across the road, must have listened for our quick knock, for sometimes she almost caught us as we ran to hide behind her azalea. But Mrs. Pearson never opened her door. Year after year, our little baskets hung on her doorknob until the lilies dangled limply and the daisies turned brown.

The year I turned ten, I begged Mother to let us pass by Mrs. Pearson's house. She just quietly shook her head. "You may not think so, but I know your baskets bring joy to that lonely old lady." So, once again, Ellen and I, holding firmly to Beth's chubby little hand, crept up to her door, knocked rather half-heartedly, and scurried behind a bush. "This is silly," I whispered to Ellen. "She never comes out."

"*Ssshhh!*" Ellen whispered fiercely, pointing toward the door as it slowly opened. A tiny, white-haired lady stepped onto the porch. She removed the Easter basket from her doorknob and sat down on the top step, our basket in her lap. Suddenly, she put her face in her hands.

"Oh dear, she's crying!" said Beth, darting out. Mother had put Beth in our charge, so Ellen and I quickly climbed up the steps after her. We found her gently patting Mrs. Pearson's shoulder.

"Are you all right?" I asked with concern.

"Yes, dear, I'm fine." she said as she looked up, wiping her cheek. "You don't know how much I love your little Easter baskets. I always leave them on the door so all the passersby can admire them." She paused and smiled shyly. "I just got a bit overwhelmed at the happy memories. You see, long ago, my sister and I used to make Easter baskets just like these."

Beth continued her patting.

"Would you girls like to come in and have

Photograph by Steve Terrill

some milk and graham crackers? I could show you pictures of when we were just about your age."

"Yes," declared Beth, marching through the open door. Since Mother had told us not to let her out of our sight, we followed.

As we sat in Mrs. Pearson's tidy little parlor eating our graham crackers, she showed us old photographs of her and her sister rolling hoops down sunlit hillsides, playing with their dolls in the woods, and best of all, proudly holding their little paper Easter baskets trimmed with long ribbons.

I wish I could say that after our visit Mrs. Pearson began tending her garden again or that she answered the door at Halloween and admired our costumes, but she didn't. Nevertheless, for the next several years, until we grew too old to weave paper baskets and hide behind lilac bushes, each Easter Day, we would climb the steps to her porch and find a little basket just for us. It was full of cookies cut in the shape of flowers. With pink frosting and sugar sprinkles.

Family Recipes

Chocolate Cream Eggs

½ cup light corn syrup
¼ cup butter, softened
1 teaspoon vanilla
¼ teaspoon salt
3 cups powdered sugar

4 drops yellow food coloring
2 drops red food coloring
1 11.5-ounce bag milk chocolate chips
2 tablespoons shortening

In a large bowl, combine corn syrup, butter, vanilla, and salt. Beat well with an electric mixer. Add powdered sugar, 1 cup at a time, mixing by hand after each addition. Remove about ⅓ of mix and place in small bowl. Add yellow and red coloring and mix well. Cover both mixes and refrigerate at least 2 hours.

When mixes are firm, roll a small ball from the orange filling and wrap around it a portion of the white filling that is twice that size. Form into the shape of an egg and place onto a greased cookie sheet. Repeat with remaining ingredients. Refrigerate 3 to 4 hours.

In a microwaveable bowl, combine chocolate chips and shortening. Microwave on high 1 minute. Stir, and microwave another minute. With a fork, dip each egg into the chocolate. Place candy on waxed paper and refrigerate 1 to 2 hours. Reheat chocolate in microwave as before, then dip each candy again. Refrigerate until completely set. Store in an airtight container. Makes 18–24 pieces.

Green Coconut Nests

1 pound white candy coating
1 7-ounce package flaked or shredded coconut
green food coloring

In a heavy saucepan over very low heat, melt coating, stirring frequently. Remove coating from heat; stir in food coloring. Add coconut; mix together well. Add very small amounts of warm water to coconut mixture until it is just thin enough to be shaped. Form into small nests by making mounds and pressing down on the centers with the bowl of a spoon. Let sit for an hour; fill with jellybeans. Makes 10–12 nests.

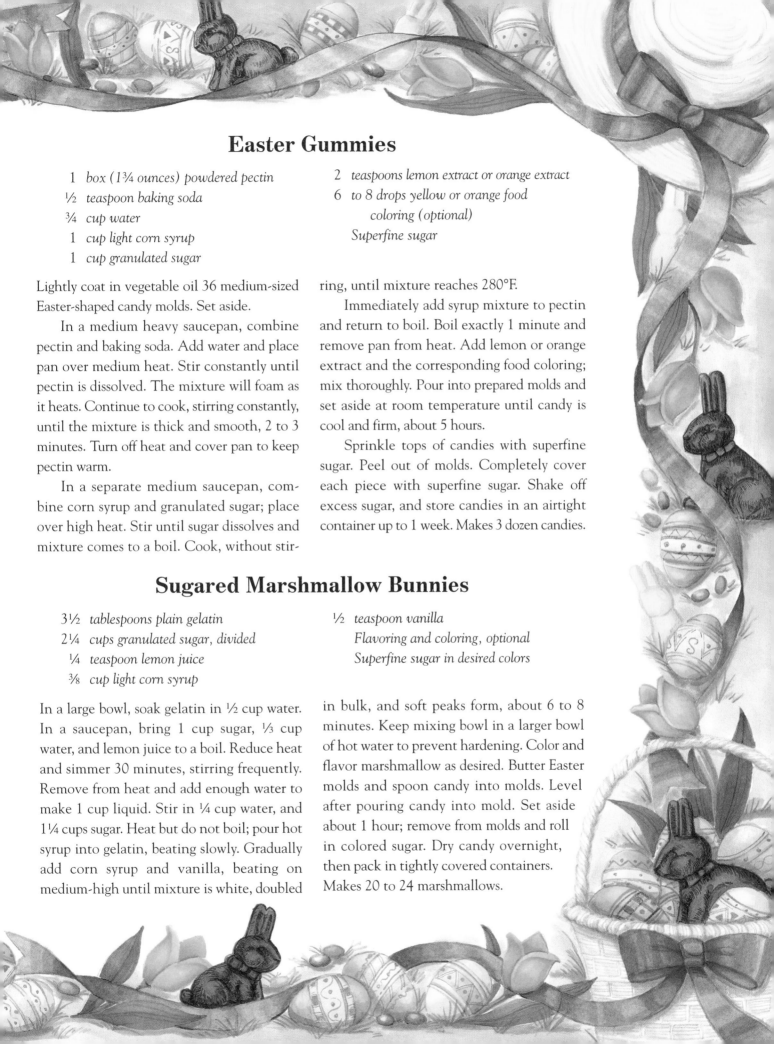

Easter Gummies

1 box (1¾ ounces) powdered pectin
½ teaspoon baking soda
¾ cup water
1 cup light corn syrup
1 cup granulated sugar

2 teaspoons lemon extract or orange extract
6 to 8 drops yellow or orange food
    coloring (optional)
    Superfine sugar

Lightly coat in vegetable oil 36 medium-sized Easter-shaped candy molds. Set aside.

In a medium heavy saucepan, combine pectin and baking soda. Add water and place pan over medium heat. Stir constantly until pectin is dissolved. The mixture will foam as it heats. Continue to cook, stirring constantly, until the mixture is thick and smooth, 2 to 3 minutes. Turn off heat and cover pan to keep pectin warm.

In a separate medium saucepan, combine corn syrup and granulated sugar; place over high heat. Stir until sugar dissolves and mixture comes to a boil. Cook, without stirring, until mixture reaches 280°F.

Immediately add syrup mixture to pectin and return to boil. Boil exactly 1 minute and remove pan from heat. Add lemon or orange extract and the corresponding food coloring; mix thoroughly. Pour into prepared molds and set aside at room temperature until candy is cool and firm, about 5 hours.

Sprinkle tops of candies with superfine sugar. Peel out of molds. Completely cover each piece with superfine sugar. Shake off excess sugar, and store candies in an airtight container up to 1 week. Makes 3 dozen candies.

Sugared Marshmallow Bunnies

3½ tablespoons plain gelatin
2¼ cups granulated sugar, divided
¼ teaspoon lemon juice
⅜ cup light corn syrup

½ teaspoon vanilla
    Flavoring and coloring, optional
    Superfine sugar in desired colors

In a large bowl, soak gelatin in ½ cup water. In a saucepan, bring 1 cup sugar, ⅓ cup water, and lemon juice to a boil. Reduce heat and simmer 30 minutes, stirring frequently. Remove from heat and add enough water to make 1 cup liquid. Stir in ¼ cup water, and 1¼ cups sugar. Heat but do not boil; pour hot syrup into gelatin, beating slowly. Gradually add corn syrup and vanilla, beating on medium-high until mixture is white, doubled in bulk, and soft peaks form, about 6 to 8 minutes. Keep mixing bowl in a larger bowl of hot water to prevent hardening. Color and flavor marshmallow as desired. Butter Easter molds and spoon candy into molds. Level after pouring candy into mold. Set aside about 1 hour; remove from molds and roll in colored sugar. Dry candy overnight, then pack in tightly covered containers. Makes 20 to 24 marshmallows.

Easter Egg Hunt

Betty Warren MacPike

I remember the Easter eggs
That were hidden here and there,
Behind the round oak table,
Under the old armchair.
Our eyes filled with excitement
As all of us scurried about,
Seeking to find bright treasures,
Laughing to bring them out.

Papa and Mama were watching,
Seeing our fun and our joy;
All of the house was shining
For each little girl and boy.
I remember those Easter egg hunts—
As if they were yesterday—
When we were carefree children
In such a heartwarming way.

Hunting Easter Eggs

Vera Laurel Hoffman

The tall green grass is bathed in sun,
Its glowing everywhere,
As little breezes move about
Like elves without a care.

The trees are showing little buds
that dance upon a bough,
Where rabbits' helpers hide bright eggs
And children hunt them now.

There's laughter in an open field
And eyes that fairly shine,
As children hunt the colored eggs
Now that it's Eastertime.

A warm and happy time of spring
When early robins sing,
When children hunt for hidden eggs—
Good things that Easter brings.

Painting by Frances Hook. Image from Ideals Publications

Easter Sunday

Deborah A. Bennett

We'd wake at sunrise and sit by the living-room window, watching the sky turn rainbow colors as night faded slowly into day. It was Easter Sunday morning, and the holiday held as many dreams for us as Christmas Day.

After the sun and Sunday breakfast, we donned our new pink taffeta dresses with white tights and patent leather shoes and purses. As we began our walk to church, there was a breeze that hinted at the warm spring breezes to come and a sweet scent in the air like yellow daffodils and purple hyacinths. A golden light filtered through the green leaves of old oaks, and the baby linden trees swayed softly in the neighbor's front yard.

It was two glorious blocks to walk, for the first time this year without our heavy winter coats and boots, hats, or scarves. Shoulder to shoulder with some, and hand in hand with others, we proudly stepped alongside our brothers and sisters and our unrecognizable friends, all dressed in their Easter finest. The girls smiled in silky ribbons and bows, white lace gloves, and Shirley Temple curls, and the boys strutted in suits and ties and fresh haircuts and mirror-like shines on their shoes.

It was a day for children's songs, particularly those we'd been practicing for weeks to sing before the Easter Sunday congregation. Choir songs and nervous little solos rang out over the smiling faces, and the room was full of streams of sunlight and the scent of Easter lilies.

After church services we hurried home to decorate the Easter eggs. Trading our Sunday silks for our Saturday gingham and the feeling of being lighter than air, we boiled and dyed and cracked and glued back together and sequined and painted and waited patiently and impatiently for those little eggs to dry. Finally we piled them in a basket to be hidden in new grass and newly green bushes for us to hunt fiercely down, like divers hunt for pearls.

Then, while washing up for dinner, we were treated to such cozy smells as baked ham and corn and sweet potatoes mixed with the hint of apple pie. We knew the freshly churned vanilla ice cream was just waiting in little blue bowls in the freezer. There was one table big enough for the entire family (and of course a few friends) to sit around. Hand in hand we said grace then spent time sharing our stories, as everybody had one, at least.

The Easter baskets waited in a pile near the hearth, like Christmas presents wait under the tree, full of little dolls and building blocks and tiny cars and Frisbees and sweet-and-sour candies and thick chocolate bunnies nestled in beds of shiny green plastic grass.

Soon we'd sit in the glow of the living-room television, watching old movies and elbowing one another for carpet space, trading jacks-and-ball sets for bags of red-hot candies, or all the black jellybeans for all the purple ones.

Photograph by Jessie Walker

It would take days to finish the chocolate bunnies. They were kept in the freezer for many an after-dinner treat. Finally only the frozen chocolate bunny feet were left for one of our "how fast can you eat your treat" contests, and then our Easter was entirely gone.

The day was the ending and the beginning of so many things for us. The ending of what pulled us in, and the beginning of what called us out. The ending of our long hibernation, and the beginning of the sky over our heads and of the grass growing beneath our feet. The ending of winter dreams and the beginning of dreams as new and green as each Easter Sunday sunrise.

Easter Morning Choir
Elizabeth Steadman Talbert

Woodland birds are singing
Resurrection lays.
Adoration winging,
Woodland birds are singing,
Lilting, tilting, swinging,
Joyously they praise.
Woodland birds are singing
Resurrection lays.

Easter Revival
Margaret Rorke

As summoned by an unseen nod,
New life is surging through the sod,
    And hope revives the heart.
Earth whispers with its warming breath,
"Behold the proof! There is no death.
    Its vestiges depart."

The feathered folk their anthems sing
To praise the miracles of spring,
    Reminding us this hour
Where rests the glory of God's plan,
Where lies the kingdom built for man,
    And where—oh, where's the power.

A Blackbird Suddenly
Joseph Auslander

Heaven is in my hand, and I
Touch a heartbeat of the sky,
Hearing a blackbird's cry.

Strange, beautiful, unquiet thing,
Lone flute of God, how can you sing
Winter to spring?

You have outdistanced every voice and word,
And given my spirit wings until it stirred
Like you—a bird!

PICKET LINE BLUES *by Susan Bourdet.*
Artwork courtesy of the artist and Wild Wings

Resurrection

Douglas Malloch

The day is Easter. Flowers bloom
On every altar. Men retell
The Resurrection from the tomb,
The tale of Christ arisen. Well,
And what means all that tale to me,
With my own cross and Calvary?

What means it all? Why, surely this:
That even as the lilies lift
Their blooms above death's dark abyss;
That even as the clouds may drift
From winter skies, the skies of March
Until the April rainbows arch;

That even as a soul may soar
From out a tomb, however barred,
And take its place forevermore
In God's eternal afterward,
So men may roll the stone away
That hides their heaven day by day.

We do not need to die to live;
We need not wait for death to rise.
Yes, even now your God will give
You certainty for some surmise
If you but ask, will let you out
From your discouragement and doubt.

The resurrection of the dead?
God grant the resurrection, too,
Of those who live! I pray instead
This day shall bring such faith to you
That you will feel in life, somehow,
Your resurrection even now.

The Triumphant Entry

Henry Vaughan

Come, drop your branches, strow the way,
Plants of the day!
Whom sufferings make most green and gay.

The King of grief, the man of sorrow
Weeping still, like the wet morrow,
Your shades and freshness comes to borrow.

Put on, put on your best array;
Let the joyed road make holy-day,
And flowers that into fields do stray,
Or secret groves, keep the high-way.

Trees, flowers, and herbs; birds, beasts, and stones,
    That since man fell, expect with groans
To see the Lamb, come, all at once,
Lift up your heads and leave your moans!
For here comes He
Whose death will be
Man's life, and your full liberty.

Hark! how the children shrill and high
Hosanna cry,
Their joys provoke the distant sky,
Where thrones and seraphim reply,
And their own angels shine and sing
In a bright ring:
Such young, sweet mirth
Makes heaven and earth
Join in a joyful symphony.

ENTRY INTO JERUSALEM *by Julius Schnorr Von Carolsfeld. Image © SuperStock, Inc./SuperStock*

Altar Lilies

Anobel Armour

No ordinary flowers are on these stems,
But pearl-white crowns, gold-studded diadems;
And He who once wore thorns upon His head
Is crowned with lovely lilies now instead.
We who receive from Him eternal spring
Have brought white crowns for Christ the King!

Eternal Spring

Mona K. Guldswog

Lilies at the altar rail on this holy Easter morn
trumpet into the waiting silence:
"Gone the darkness! Gone the storm!
He lives! Christ lives! New hope is born!"
Candles catch the flame of faith and steadfastly burn.
Each heart lifts, the blessed assurance
brightening regions that were dim.
Perhaps all strife and cares might yet one day
be overcome and peace return.
The message is proclaimed not only from
cathedrals with stately spires and pealing bells,
but in each tender shoot along the lowliest of roads
refusing to accept the earth's hard crust,
pushing upwards to reach the sun,
one more witness to foretell
the joy of eternal spring.

Photograph by William H. Johnson

For God So Loved the World

John 3:1–21

There was a man of the Pharisees, named Nicodemus, a ruler of the Jews: The same came to Jesus by night, and said unto him, Rabbi, we know that thou art a teacher come from God: for no man can do these miracles that thou doest, except God be with him.

Jesus answered and said unto him, Verily, verily, I say unto thee, Except a man be born again, he cannot see the kingdom of God.

Nicodemus saith unto him, How can a man be born when he is old? can he enter the second time into his mother's womb, and be born?

Jesus answered, Verily, verily, I say unto thee, Except a man be born of water and of the Spirit, he cannot enter into the kingdom of God.

That which is born of the flesh is flesh; and that which is born of the Spirit is spirit. Marvel not that I said unto thee, Ye must be born again. The wind bloweth where it listeth, and thou hearest the sound thereof, but canst not tell whence it cometh, and whither it goeth: so is every one that is born of the Spirit.

Nicodemus answered and said unto him, How can these things be?

Jesus answered and said unto him, Art thou a master of Israel, and knowest not these things? Verily, verily, I say unto thee, We speak that we do know, and testify that we have seen; and ye receive not our witness.

If I have told you earthly things, and ye believe not, how shall ye believe, if I tell you of heavenly things? And no man hath ascended up to heaven, but he that came down from heaven, even the Son of man which is in heaven. And as Moses lifted up the serpent in the wilderness, even so must the Son of man be lifted up: That whosoever believeth in him should not perish, but have eternal life.

For God so loved the world, that he gave his only begotten Son, that whosoever believeth in him should not perish, but have everlasting life. For God sent not his Son into the world to condemn the world; but that the world through him might be saved.

He that believeth on him is not condemned: but he that believeth not is condemned already, because he hath not believed in the name of the only begotten Son of God. And this is the condemnation, that light is come into the world, and men loved darkness rather than light, because their deeds were evil. For every one that doeth evil hateth the light, neither cometh to the light, lest his deeds should be reproved.

But he that doeth truth cometh to the light, that his deeds may be made manifest, that they are wrought in God.

Beneath the Cross

John 19:25–42

Now there stood by the cross of Jesus his mother, and his mother's sister, Mary the wife of Cleophas, and Mary Magdalene.

When Jesus therefore saw his mother, and the disciple standing by, whom he loved, he saith unto his mother, Woman, behold thy son!

Then saith he to the disciple, Behold thy mother! And from that hour that disciple took her unto his own home.

After this, Jesus knowing that all things were now accomplished, that the scripture might be fulfilled, saith, I thirst. Now there was set a vessel full of vinegar: and they filled a spunge with vinegar, and put it upon hyssop, and put it to his mouth.

When Jesus therefore had received the vinegar, he said, It is finished: and he bowed his head, and gave up the ghost.

The Jews therefore, because it was the preparation, that the bodies should not remain upon the cross on the sabbath day, (for that sabbath day was an high day,) besought Pilate that their legs might be broken, and that they might be taken away. Then came the soldiers, and brake the legs of the first, and of the other which was crucified with him. But when they came to Jesus, and saw that he was dead already, they brake not his legs: But one of the soldiers with a spear pierced his side, and forthwith came there out blood and water.

And he that saw it bare record, and his record is true: and he knoweth that he saith true, that ye might believe. For these things were done, that the scripture should be fulfilled, A bone of him shall not be broken. And again another scripture saith, They shall look on him whom they pierced.

And after this Joseph of Arimathaea, being a disciple of Jesus, but secretly for fear of the Jews, besought Pilate that he might take away the body of Jesus: and Pilate gave him leave. He came therefore, and took the body of Jesus.

And there came also Nicodemus, which at the first came to Jesus by night, and brought a mixture of myrrh and aloes, about an hundred pound weight.

Then took they the body of Jesus, and wound it in linen clothes with the spices, as the manner of the Jews is to bury.

Now in the place where he was crucified there was a garden; and in the garden a new sepulchre, wherein was never man yet laid.

There laid they Jesus therefore because of the Jews' preparation day; for the sepulchre was nigh at hand.

The Stone Rolled Away

Mark 16:1–15

And when the sabbath was past, Mary Magdalene, and Mary the mother of James, and Salome, had bought sweet spices, that they might come and anoint him.

And very early in the morning the first day of the week, they came unto the sepulchre at the rising of the sun. And they said among themselves, Who shall roll us away the stone from the door of the sepulchre?

And when they looked, they saw that the stone was rolled away: for it was very great.

And entering into the sepulchre, they saw a young man sitting on the right side, clothed in a long white garment; and they were affrighted.

And he saith unto them, Be not affrighted: Ye seek Jesus of Nazareth, which was crucified: he is risen; he is not here: behold the place where they laid him.

But go your way, tell his disciples and Peter that he goeth before you into Galilee: there shall ye see him, as he said unto you.

And they went out quickly, and fled from the sepulchre; for they trembled and were amazed: neither said they any thing to any man; for they were afraid.

Now when Jesus was risen early the first day of the week, he appeared first to Mary Magdalene, out of whom he had cast seven devils.

And she went and told them that had been with him, as they mourned and wept.

And they, when they had heard that he was alive, and had been seen of her, believed not.

After that he appeared in another form unto two of them, as they walked, and went into the country.

And they went and told it unto the residue: neither believed they them.

Afterward he appeared unto the eleven as they sat at meat, and upbraided them with their unbelief and hardness of heart, because they believed not them which had seen him after he was risen.

And he said unto them, Go ye into all the world, and preach the gospel to every creature.

Easter Morning
Phillips Brooks

Tomb, thou shalt not hold Him longer—
Death is strong, but life is stronger;
Stronger than the dark, the light;
Stronger than the wrong, the right.
Faith and hope triumphant say,
"Christ will rise on Easter Day!"

While the patient Earth lies waking
Till the morning shall be breaking,
Shuddering 'neath the burden dread
Of her Master, cold and dead,
Hark! she hears the angels say,
"Christ will rise on Easter Day!"

And when sunrise smites the mountains,
Pouring light from heavenly fountains,
Then the Earth blooms out to greet
Once again the blessed feet;
And her countless voices say,
"Christ has risen on Easter Day!"

✝ Him Evermore I Behold
Henry Wadsworth Longfellow

Him evermore I behold
Walking in Galilee,
Through the cornfield's
 waving gold,
In hamlet or grassy wold,
By the shores of the beautiful sea.
He toucheth the sightless eyes;

Before Him the demons flee;
To the dead He sayeth, Arise!
To the living, Follow me!
And that voice still
 soundeth on
From the centuries that are gone
To the centuries that shall be!

Pre-dawn light on Tatoosh Range of
Mount Rainier National Park, Washington.
Photograph by Mary Liz Austin/Austin Donnelly Photography

THROUGH MY WINDOW

Nicodemus: A Resurrection Story

Pamela Kennedy

It was the evening of the first day of the week. Nicodemus sat in the courtyard of his home listening to the rustle of leaves and the scuttling sounds of chameleons chasing insects. Overhead, the stars sparkled, individual pinpricks in the dark fabric of sky. It was late, but he could not sleep. His mind tumbled over and over the words of the women: "Jesus lives. He is not in the tomb. He has risen!"

How could it be? Just three days earlier, on the evening prior to the Sabbath, Nicodemus and his fellow Pharisee, Joseph of Arimathea, had begged Jesus' dead body from Pilate. Nicodemus had purchased with his own money an embalming mixture of myrrh and aloes, seventy-five pounds worth. Joseph and he had wrapped the body with clean strips of linen, packing the precious spices in the folds. Then they had carried the prepared body to Joseph's tomb in the garden outside Jerusalem. Nicodemus could still feel the weight of their burden as they hurried through the streets. Tenderly, they had laid their Teacher on the rough-hewn slab. Then they left, sealing the tomb from grave robbers with a huge stone. Nicodemus remembered it all in vivid detail. He was a man of learning, a Pharisee, but even the simplest person knows that dead people do not live again.

Then words sprang to mind, words Jesus had spoken to him months earlier: "You must be born again." And Nicodemus remembered his response: "That's impossible. How can a person who is old enter once again into his mother's womb?" Jesus had looked at him then as one might gaze at a little child. Gently, He had instructed the Jewish teacher, weaving together words about wind and spirit. Then He had rebuked Nicodemus as if he were a teacher without learning who, because he could not comprehend earthly things, would never be able to grasp the truths of heaven. The words stung. Nicodemus had realized that despite all his learning, years spent memorizing and debating the Scriptures, he was still ignorant of the things that he most longed to know. He felt condemned. And that was when Jesus had made His most amazing statement. Placing His hand on the shoulder of the Pharisee, He had spoken of God's love—a love so amazing that it had compelled the ruler of the universe to enter time and space, to reveal Himself to humankind, to offer reconciliation and redemption to whomever chose to believe in Him. It was inconceivable, impossible . . . as impossible as a dead body coming back to life.

Nicodemus drew in his breath sharply. That was it! The key to the whole mystery of this man who had so captivated him. He wasn't merely

another good teacher, a learned rabbi, a worker of miracles. He was indeed who He had said. He was the one and only Son of God. Now the words about being born again made sense. It wasn't about wombs and years; it was about spirit and eternity.

Suddenly, the preposterous message of the women seemed more real than the stones under his feet. Nicodemus lifted his arms and looked at his hands. He had held the Son of God in these arms, used these fingers to tenderly fold linens and spices around His bruised body. Yet now he recognized that his actions had more to do with a birth than a burial. Jesus was not about death, but about life, just as He had said.

In the same way he had experienced the physical release of the weight of Jesus' embalmed body a few days earlier, the Pharisee now experienced the release of a far greater weight. Fear, obsessive doubts, and never-ending feelings of failure lifted from his heart like the smoke rising from the incense in the temple. In their place the freshening wind of new life and hope rushed in.

Speechless, Nicodemus bowed his head for a few moments then raised his face to the night sky. Through his tears the stars wove their light together into a gleaming tapestry. Finally he raised his empty hands and whispered the only prayer that now seemed adequate, "Thank You, Father."

The Resurrection

Jonathan Henderson Brooks

His friends went off and left Him dead
In Joseph's subterranean bed,
Embalmed with myrrh and sweet aloes
And wrapped in snow-white burial clothes.

Then shrewd men came and set a seal
Upon His grave, lest thieves should steal
His lifeless form away and claim
For Him an undeserving fame.

"There is no use," the soldiers said,
"Of standing sentries by the dead."
Wherefore, they drew their cloaks around
Themselves, and fell upon the ground
And slept like dead men, all night through,
In the pale moonlight and chilling dew.

A muffled whiff of sudden breath
Ruffled the passive air of death.

He woke and raised Himself in bed,
Recalled how He was crucified;
Touched both hands, fingers to
  His head,
And lightly felt His fresh-healed side.

Then with a deep, triumphant sigh,
He cooly put His grave-clothes by—
Folded the sweet, white winding sheet,
The toweling, the linen bands,
The napkin, all with careful hands—
And left the burrowed chamber neat.

His steps were like the breaking day:
So soft across the watch He stole,
He did not wake a single soul,
Nor spill one dewdrop by the way.

Now Calvary was loveliness:
Lilies that flowered thereupon
Pulled off the white moon's pallid dress
And put the morning's vesture on.

"Why seek the living among the dead?
He is not here," the angel said.

The early winds took up the words
And bore them to the lilting birds,
The leafing trees, and everything
That breathed the living
  breath of spring.

Photograph by Terry Donnelly/Austin Donnelly Photography

from **The Easter Joy**

Margaret E. Sangster

Once more with flowers and hymns of praise we enter our holy places; once more we hear sounding over every open grave, and hushing every rebellious thought in our hearts and soothing every grief, the words of Him who still says to every one of us, "I am the Resurrection and the Life; he that believeth in Me, though he were dead yet shall he live." Because our blessed Captain tasted death for every one of us, and Himself took on His pale lips its utmost bitterness, the cup which the death angel holds to our lips is filled with the sweetness and flavor of everlasting life. This is the great joy of Easter. More and more, as we go on traveling the pilgrim road, we are conscious that it is but a road leading to another and an endless home. Along the road there are beautiful surprises. Friendship is ours, and domestic bliss; the dear love of kindred; the sweetness of companionship; the delight of standing shoulder to shoulder with comrades; the glory of service. But this is not our rest, and we are going on to that place where the beloved of the Lord shall dwell in safety by Him and where they go no more out forever.

Somehow Easter always carries with it more of heaven than any other of the great anniversaries of the Christian year. In its first bright dawn the heavens were opened and the angels came down to comfort the weeping women and the disciples, mourning their Lord at the sepulcher, with those ecstatic words, "He is not here; He is risen!" It is more than fancy, it is a precious fact, that the angels still come back to console the mourner, to strengthen the doubting, and to give Christ's own people the blessed assurance that He is with them still.

The festival of Easter comes to us at a propitious time, for lo, the winter is past, the rain is over and gone, the flowers appear on the earth, the time of the singing of birds is come, and the voice of the turtle is heard in our land. Winter, with its rigor and cold, its ice and frost and inclement blasts, its tempests on land and sea, is an emblem of warfare; its silence and sternness ally it to grief. Spring comes dancing and fluttering in with flowers and music and the blithe step of childhood. Her signs are evident before she is really here herself. First come the bluebirds, harbingers of a host; a little later there will be wrens and robins and orioles, and all the troop which makes the woods musical and builds sociably around our country homes.

Then the flowers will come. Happy are they who shall watch their whole procession, from the pussy willow in March to the last blue gentian in October. We decorate our churches at Easter with the finest spoils of the hothouse—lilies, roses, palms, azaleas; nothing is too costly, nothing too lavish to be brought to the sanctuary or carried to the cemetery. Friend sends to friend the fragrant bouquet or the growing plant with the same tender significance which is evinced in the Christmas gifts, which carry from one heart to another a sweet message of love.

But God is giving us the Easter flowers in little hidden nooks in the forests, down by the corners of fences, in the sheltered places on the edges of the brook, and there we find the violet, the arbutus and other delicate blossoms which lead the van for the great army of nature's efflorescence. The first flowers are more delicately tinted and of shyer look and more ephemeral fragrance than those which come later. They are the Easter flowers. Later on we shall have millions of blossoms and more birds than we can count. Now in the garden and the field we have enough to remind us that the winter is past, the rain is over and gone, the time of the singing of birds is come.

If any of us have been grieving over our own lack, over our sinful departure from God, or over the loss of dear ones, let us at Easter forget the past, put our hand in that of our risen Lord, accept the sweetness of His voice and the gladness of His presence as He comes into our homes, and say, thankfully, as we hear His "Peace be unto you": "Lord, we are Thine at this Easter time; we give ourselves to Thee in a fullness which we have never known before. We are Thine. Thine to use as Thou wilt; Thine to fill with blessing; Thine to own. Take us, Lord, and so possess us with Thyself that our waste places shall be glad and the wilderness of our lives shall blossom as the rose." Such a prayer will find its way upward and return to us in wonderful answers of blessing from the Lord.

Photograph by Terry Donnelly/
Austin Donnelly Photography

Dawn

Margaret Rorke

At dawn on that first Easter Day,
An angel rolled the stone away
And waited for the three
Who came with trembling fear and dread
To lovingly anoint the Dead,
But dawn had found Him free.

That dawn's great resurrection light
Awakened those who had the sight
To see His truth revealed.

They grasped the answer granted grief.
They sensed the power of belief.
All this the dawn unsealed.

That dawn there was a great rebirth
Of what would make a better earth
According to God's plan.
May we this Easter Day awake
With resurrected zeal to make
A brighter dawn for man.

Once in a Garden

Grace Noll Crowell

Once in a garden while it was yet dark,
A woman walked the flower-bordered way—
Her garments trailing, in her hands she bore
Sweet-smelling spices for her Lord that day.
Gray olives dropped their heavy shadows down
Across a path familiar to her feet;
A broken flower, bruised beneath her tread,
Gave up its incense, fragrant, dewy-sweet.
Close in the dusk arose the sepulcher;
Ah, still the beating heart, the stone is gone!
"They have taken Him away—my Lord, my Lord!"
Poor troubled heart, this hour before the dawn.
Once in an old-time garden of the world
It happened thus—'twas darkest, deepest night,
And lo, across the east there kindled, flamed,
One radiant heavenly light.

"Whom seekest thou?" Ah, whom
    but Thee, dear Lord?
"Why weepest thou?" Dear heart,
    from sorrow freed,
Forget thy grief, look up,
    and laugh and sing:
The Lord is risen indeed.

Oaks and boulders in central California foothills. Photograph by Carr Clifton

Resurrection Day
Leon Eugene Wright

The dazzling rays of light today
Disperse the cold and gloom.
The shortening shadows seem to say,
"Come forth ye from the tomb.
This is your resurrection day;
Let springtime flowers bloom.
The birds shall sing their songs, so gay;
All nature shall resume
Her healing growth from earthy clay
And scatter sweet perfume."

FROM An Easter Canticle
Charles Hanson Towne

In every trembling bud and bloom
That cleaves the earth, a flowery sword,
I see Thee come from out the tomb,
Thou risen Lord.

Thou art not dead! Thou art the whole
Of life that quickens in the sod;
Green April is Thy very soul,
Thou great Lord God.

IF THIS BRIGHT LILY
CAN LIVE ONCE MORE,
AS ITS WHITE PROMISE
BE AS BEFORE,
WHY CAN NOT
THE GREAT STONE
BE MOVED FROM HIS DOOR?
—Charles Hanson Towne

Anza-Borrego Desert State Park, California.
Photograph by Mary Liz Austin/Austin Donnelly Photography

Christ, the Lord, Is Risen Today

Charles Wesley

Christ, the Lord, is risen today, Alleluia!
Sons of men and angels say, Alleluia!
Raise your joys and triumphs high, Alleluia!
Sing, ye heavens and earth reply, Alleluia!

Love's redeeming work is done, Alleluia!
Fought the fight, the battle won, Alleluia!
Lo! the sun's eclipse is o'er, Alleluia!
Lo! He sets in blood no more, Alleluia!

Vain the stone, the watch, the seal, Alleluia!
Christ hath burst the gates of hell, Alleluia!
Death in vain forbids His rise, Alleluia!
Christ hath opened paradise, Alleluia!

Lives again our glorious King, Alleluia!
Where, O death, is now thy sting? Alleluia!
Once He died our souls to save, Alleluia!
Where thy victory, O grave? Alleluia!

Soar we now where Christ hath led, Alleluia!
Following our exalted Head, Alleluia!
Made like Him, like Him we rise, Alleluia!
Ours the cross, the grave, the skies, Alleluia!

Hail, the Lord of earth and heaven, Alleluia!
Praise to Thee by both be given, Alleluia!
Thee we greet triumphant now, Alleluia!
Hail, the Resurrection, thou, Alleluia!

King of glory, Soul of bliss, Alleluia!
Everlasting life is this, Alleluia!
Thee to know, Thy power to prove, Alleluia!
Thus to sing and thus to love, Alleluia!

Hymns of praise then let us sing, Alleluia!
Unto Christ, our heavenly King, Alleluia!
Who endured the cross and grave, Alleluia!
Sinners to redeem and save, Alleluia!

But the pains that He endured, Alleluia!
Our salvation have procured, Alleluia!
Now above the sky He's King, Alleluia!
Where the angels ever sing. Alleluia!

Jesus Christ is risen today, Alleluia!
Our triumphant holy day, Alleluia!
Who did once upon the cross, Alleluia!
Suffer to redeem our loss. Alleluia!

Grange church with dogwood tree. Photograph by
William H. Johnson

Cross Purposes

Pamela Kennedy

For many people today, the cross is a wardrobe accessory. Necklaces, earrings, and T-shirts featuring crosses are commonplace. But for George Bennard, an officer in the Salvation Army and a traveling Methodist evangelist, the cross was much more than an adornment or a sentimental symbol.

It was 1913 and Bennard had just completed an exhausting round of revival meetings in New York. Returning home to Michigan, he engaged in a time of rest and reflection. Searching the Scriptures, as he often did when faced with challenges, the evangelist happened upon the letter from Paul to the Galatians. In the sixth chapter he read, "May I never boast except in the cross of our Lord Jesus Christ, through which the world has been crucified to me, and I to the world." Meditating upon this passage, Bennard realized that the cross was not merely a symbol of his faith, but the very linchpin of it. In his writings, he reports that during this time, the phrase "the old rugged cross" came repeatedly to mind. Then, as he continued to ponder these four words, a few notes of melody seemed to echo in his head. Quickly, he wrote them down. It would be a few more weeks before he completed the four verses and chorus of the hymn we now know as "The Old Rugged Cross"; but he said that after much prayer, the words finally began to come, and they flowed from his pen almost unbidden.

He shared the completed hymn first with a few friends and then at the Chicago Evangelistic Institute, where the response was enthusiastic. Encouraged by a leading gospel hymn composer, Charles Gabriel, and sponsored by a fellow pastor, Bennard published the hymn shortly after its composition. Within a brief period of time it was outselling every other sacred and secular song in the country. Before the mid-twentieth century, more than twenty million copies had been published; and even today, "The Old Rugged Cross" is a perennial favorite in hymnals and gospel songbooks, in church services, and in evangelistic meetings.

Bennard would write other hymns during his lifetime, but none would ever reach the popularity of his first. In 1958, at the age of eighty-five, he finally "exchanged his cross for a crown." The city fathers in his hometown of Reed City, Michigan, wanted to erect a memorial in his honor. Eschewing more traditional monuments and statues, they chose something far more appropriate. Near the house where George Bennard died, they erected a twelve-foot-high wooden cross. On it is a plaque that reads: "'The Old Rugged Cross'—Home of George Bennard, composer of the beloved hymn." One can't help but feel that Bennard would have approved. For him, the purpose of the cross had at last been realized.

The Old Rugged Cross

Words and lyrics by George Bennard

On a hill far a-way stood an old rug-ged cross, The em-blem of
suf-f'ring and shame. And I love that old cross where the
dear-est and best For a world of lost sin-ners was slain.
So I'll cher-ish the old rug-ged cross, Till my
tro-phies at last I lay down; I will cling to the old rug-ged
cross, And ex-change it some day for a crown.

Walk to Emmaus

Luke 24:13–17, 19b–21, 23, 25–32

And, behold, two of them went that same day to a village called Emmaus, which was from Jerusalem about threescore furlongs. And they talked together of all these things which had happened. And it came to pass, that, while they communed together and reasoned, Jesus himself drew near, and went with them. But their eyes were holden that they should not know him.

And he said unto them, What manner of communications are these that ye have one to another, as ye walk, and are sad? . . .

And they said unto him, Concerning Jesus of Nazareth, which was a prophet mighty in deed and word before God and all the people: And how the chief priests and our rulers delivered him to be condemned to death, and have crucified him. But we trusted that it had been he which should have redeemed Israel: and beside all this, to day is the third day since these things were done. . . . And when they found not his body, they came, saying, that they had also seen a vision of angels, which said that he was alive. . . .

Then he said unto them, O fools, and slow of heart to believe all that the prophets have spoken: Ought not Christ to have suffered these things, and to enter into his glory? And beginning at Moses and all the prophets, he expounded unto them in all the scriptures the things concerning himself.

And they drew nigh unto the village, whither they went: and he made as though he would have gone further. But they constrained him, saying, Abide with us: for it is toward evening, and the day is far spent. And he went in to tarry with them.

And it came to pass, as he sat at meat with them, he took bread, and blessed it, and brake, and gave to them. And their eyes were opened, and they knew him; and he vanished out of their sight.

And they said one to another, Did not our heart burn within us, while he talked with us by the way, and while he opened to us the scriptures?

Emmaus Road

Margaret Rorke

Christ walked with two
Who knew Him well
Along that dusty path.
What He'd been through
He heard them tell:
His death and aftermath.
Confused, bereft,
Bowed down with grief—
Their eyes upon the soil,

What had they left
But mixed belief
In Him they thought was royal?
They argued some
As they conversed
Upon that Easter Day
'Bout Him who'd come
And known man's worst,
But failed to look His way.

Make me wide-eyed
That I may know,
Though heavy be my load,
He's at my side
The while I go
Down my Emmaus Road.

National Arboretum, Washington DC.
Photograph by Mary Liz Austin/Austin Donnelly Photography

Featured Poet

Risen

Eileen Spinelli

Spring hills beckon
sudden green.
Sun has risen
once again.
Easter morning—
swimming light
in the sea-sky,
birdsong bright.
Birdsong . . .
beesong . . .
heartsong . . .
new.
Hope—
once fragile—
billows true.
Darkness fades
beyond the gate.
Son is risen:
celebrate!

SPRING GARDEN—BABY ROBINS *by Susan Bourdet.*
Artwork courtesy of the artist and Wild Wings

There Is Always Hope

Daniel Schantz

What a joy it must have been for Jesus to appear to His friends after His Resurrection. I see this joy coming out in the covert encounter with two discouraged disciples who were shuffling their way toward Emmaus. Incognito, Jesus joins them and pretends not to know what they are talking about. "What things?" He asks, as if He didn't know. He listens sympathetically and reminds them of some scriptures they had overlooked. When, at last, He reveals Himself, their hearts once again burn with hope.

It's all too easy to lose hope in this life, I think. That dream job gets put on the back burner because you need cash now. The handsome prince you married turns out to be a toad. Someone else bought the split-level you wanted, and college plans were set aside when the children came along.

The Resurrection of Christ is a wake-up call for my sidetracked yearnings. When God is involved, there is always hope. Hope is not just a noun, it's also a verb—something I should practice, like Abraham, who "hoped against hope" (Romans 4:18).

Perhaps God has already set in motion forces that will even yet bring my dreams to pass. Maybe, when children are grown, college will be even sweeter. That split-level might come up for sale again, at a better time. That hubby might just need time to find his princely side. And that current job might be a steppingstone to more stellar assignments.

Today, the anniversary of death's defeat, would be a good time to dust off one of those dreams and present it to the Lord of hope.

Oak branches in the spring, in Great Smoky Mountains National Park, Tennessee. Photograph by William H. Johnson

Therefore we are buried with him by baptism into death: that like as Christ was raised up from the dead by the glory of the Father, even so we also should walk in newness of life. —Romans 6:4

Spring Thoughts

Ellen Sue Waigle

I looked into a flower
So delicate and fair;
And as I looked, I thought I saw
The face of Jesus there.

I listened to a singing bird
Perched high within a tree,
And as I listened, thought I heard
My Jesus speak to me.

I wandered through the cool
   spring woods,
New beauty everywhere,
And as I walked I thought I felt
The Savior's presence there.

TRILLIUM

Photograph by William H. Johnson

Again

Mary Stoner Wine

Again the brown, bare earth is green;
The flowers and bursting buds are seen.
The robins and the redbirds sing,
And nature blooms in glorious spring.

Again we go with Christ through days
When friends forsake, and all His ways
Are paths of sorrow and defeat
Till death makes sacrifice complete.

Again we stand beside the tomb
And contemplate its cold, damp gloom.
But even there a hope is born
Of life and resurrection morn.

Again our faith most surely knows
That Christ, the Lord, from death arose;
It conquers doubts that would destroy
And sings in glad, triumphant joy.

Promise

Scott Horton

Deep in the earth a seedling
Pushing toward the light,
Lifting up to the sunshine,
Up from the long dark night.

Deep in the heart a longing,
A hope that is dearer far
Than life, of home lights burning
And gates that stand ajar.

Deep in the tomb a promise
Cloistered from the day.
Oh, faint hearts, be courageous;
He rolled the stone away.

Photograph by William H. Johnson

*A*S THE DEWDROPS SHIMMER
ON THE WINGS OF THE BUTTERFLY,
MY HEART SMILES TO KNOW
THE PROMISE OF SPRING
IS FULFILLED.
—*Author Unknown*

ISBN-13: 978-0-8249-1321-2

Published by Ideals Publications, a Guideposts Company
Nashville, Tennessee
www.idealsbooks.com

Publisher, Peggy Schaefer
Editor, Melinda Rathjen
Copy Editor, Michelle Prater Burke
Designer, Marisa Jackson
Permissions Editor, Patsy Jay

Cover: Photograph by William H. Johnson
Inside front cover: Painting by Donald Mills. Image from Ideals Publications
Inside back cover: Painting by T. Hoffman. Image from Ideals Publications
Additional Art Credits: "Bits & Pieces" art by Kathy Rusynyk; "Family Recipes" art by Stacy Venturi-Pickett; "The Old Rugged Cross" arranged and set by Dick Torrans; *Heavy Downpour* by Rollie Brandt, *Picket Line Blues* and *Spring Garden—Baby Robins* by Susan Bourdet, courtesy of the artists and Wild Wings (www.wildwings.com)

ACKNOWLEDGMENTS:

AUSLANDER, JOSEPH. "A Blackbird Suddenly." Originally published in *The Ladies Home Journal* by The Meredith Corporation. BROOKS, JONATHAN HENDERSON. "The Resurrection" from *The Resurrection and Other Poems*, by Jonathan Henderson Brooks. Published by Kaleidograph Press, 1948. CROWELL, GRACE NOLL. "Once in a Garden" from *Let the Sun Shine In* by Grace Noll Crowell. Copyright © 1970. Used by permission of Fleming Revell, a division of Baker Publishing Group. GINSBERG, LOUIS. "Spring Violets" from *The Everlasting Minute*. Published in 1937 by Liveright Publication, W. W. Norton & Company. MALLOCH, DOUGLAS. "Resurrection." Used by permission of Lareda Anderson. RORKE, MARGARET L. "Easter" and "Dawn" and "Emmaus Road" from *An Old Cracked Cup*. Copyright © 1980 by the author. Published by Northwood Institute Press. Used by permis-sion of Margaret Ann Rorke. SCHANTZ, DANIEL. "There Is Always Hope" from *Daily Guideposts 2003*. Copyright © 2002 by Guideposts. All rights reserved. STOREY,

VIOLET ALLEYN. "On Planting a Tulip Bulb" from *A Poet Prays* by Violet Alleyn Storey. Copyright © 1959 by Abingdon Press and used with their permission.

Our thanks to the following authors or their heirs: Faith Andrews Bedford, George Bennard, Deborah A. Bennett, Thomas Curtis Clark, Christine Deeren, Loise Pinkerton Fritz, Mona K. Guldswog, Kay Hoffman, Vera Laurel Hoffman, Scott Horton, Frances Kampman, Pamela Kennedy, Betty Warren MacPike, Alice Leedy Mason, Gail L. Roberson, Eileen Spinelli, Elizabeth Steadman Talbert, Ellen Sue Waigle, May Smith White, Mary Stoner Wine, Leon Eugene Wright.

Every effort has been made to establish ownership and use of each selection in this book. If contacted, the publisher will be pleased to rectify any inadvertent errors or omissions in subsequent editions.